LOCATION

LOCATION

LOCATION

While this booklet refers to opening
a Wild Bird Retail Store its contents
are applicable to most any retail store.

This guide was developed by
International Business Location Advisors.
It has been copied and modified with the
copyright owners permission by
John F. Gardner

Table of Contents

Location, Location, Location

What are the three most important characteristics to consider when choosing the right location for your business? Location, location, location! Perhaps you've heard this before. But until now, very little has been shared about what a strong location *really* is and why its characteristics should be carefully considered. In the retail industry a strong location means that a store can realize its full sales potential. Industry examples show that strong locations increase gross sales by more than 100%. Similarly, weak locations yield lethargic sales performances of half of a concept's potential. McDonald's restaurants for example, average $1.9 million a year in gross sales per restaurant. But the sales levels from one McDonald's restaurant to another varies from $500,000 to $2.5 million. In comparing one McDonald's to another, we know that the food is the same, the menu is the same, the prices are the same, and the buildings look the same. So what accounts for this huge difference in volume? The answer is "Location".

Preface

The following guide is a step by step look at a process similar to what some of the largest and fastest growing retailers in the world use to select their own real estate locations. Between the top growth companies over 1,000,000 new stores have been built nationwide during the past three decades. The experience gained through this tremendous 30 year expansion has created what is now a very clear process to finding successful locations.

The great news associated with this process is you don't have to be a big company or invest a large sum of money to use it. The process is both easy to learn and implement. Entrepreneurs with a dream of opening a wild bird store can insure that they are choosing the strongest location for their store so that they can realize their highest sales potential.

This workbook will guide you step by step through a process that will help you select the strongest location for your store. We start by describing the most common mistake made by those seeking out a location. This serves as an introduction for the layout of the body of the book.

Chapter 1
Discusses macro area issues like which part of an area should one begin the search for a location. It provides sources of information to help you make this decision, based an a number of data points. Chances are that you have already decided upon your general area; in this case, this chapter will serve more as a verification of your selected market.

Chapter 2
Defines the "trade area" in detail and will help equip you with all you need to know about how to analyze trade area characteristics.

Chapter 3
Describes how to identify actual trade areas, as well as how to gather information you will need from various sources.

Chapter 4

Defines the eight elements of a site and outlines how to find sites in identified trade areas.

Chapter 5

Describes some legal clauses that are of particular importance in maintaining your business's strong location.

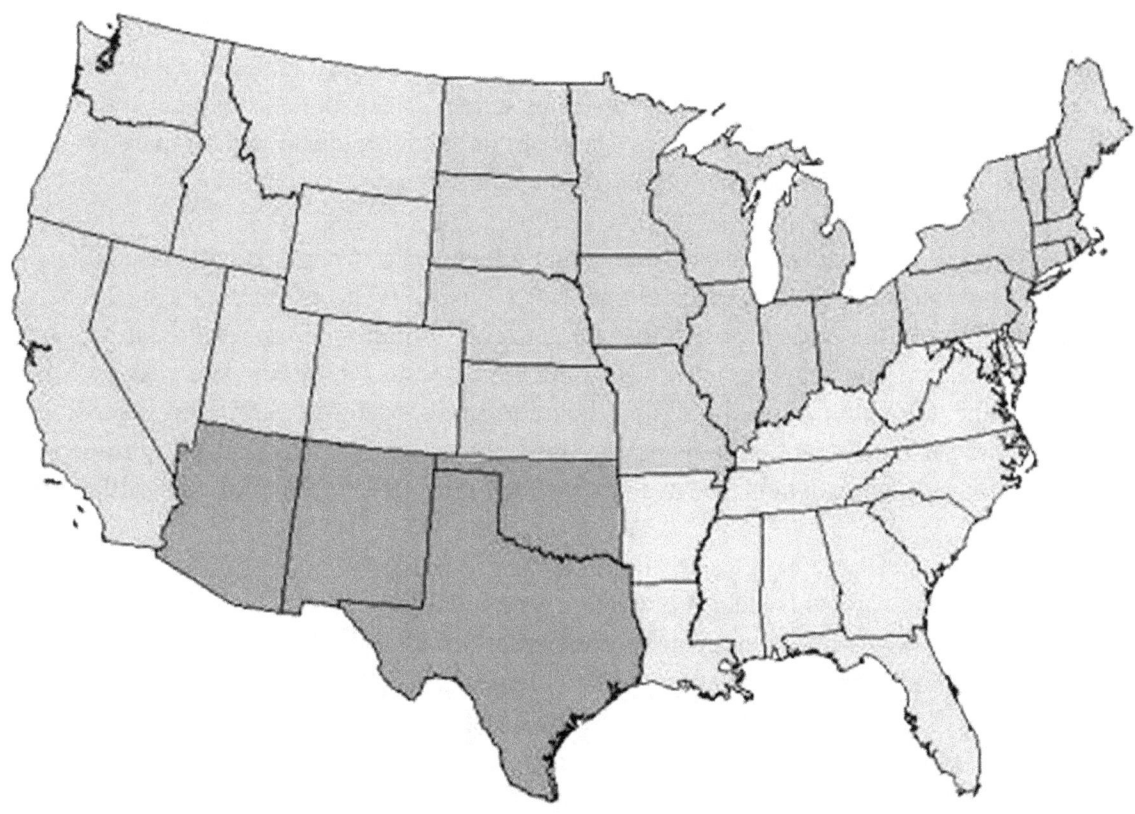

Introduction

The most common mistake made when looking for a site is to find one "that looks like a real winner" and then proceed to justify the characteristics of the area in which it is located. The correct way to find a site is first to identify areas that exceed certain benchmark criteria, then rank these areas based on the criteria and finally locate possible sites within the highest ranking areas. The areas that are examined are called trade areas. Trade areas are an important concept to understand and are defined in Chapter 2.

The subtle difference of reversing the steps of area identification and site identification will allow you to more efficiently find a location that will maximize your concepts sales potential. The example below highlights why this is the case.

Example:
Consider a corner site at a light in front of a grocery store shopping center. Further consider that the site has good visibility and access. From the stand point of specific site characteristics the location appears fairly good. Now assume that the grocery store is the smaller, less vibrant of two grocery stores which service surrounding neighborhoods. The shopping centers compete for customers and by viewing the number of cars in the parking lot throughout the day, this center is clearly less vibrant in comparison to the competing center. Consider an identical site in the vicinity of the more vibrant shopping center. This site is obviously more desirable compared to the initial site because of the increased number of people that shop there.

The key to keep in mind in this example is that a location's strength is comprised of two sets of elements. The first is the site's specific elements (i.e. visibility, access and parking). The second is the characteristics of the trade area that the site is in (i.e. vibrancy of the retail centers, growth and demographics). The two together make up a location. Because a specific site always falls within a trade area, the site's strength is limited by the trade area's strength. So finding a great site in a poor trade area yields a location that is poor. Similarly an average site in a strong trade area yields a good location, and an excellent site in a strong trade area yields a location that will maximize your business's sales.

Given this framework, it is clear that the first step in looking for the right location is to identify strong trade areas. Only after a number of trade areas are identified, analyzed and prioritized, should specific sites be identified. The result will be to choose among different sites, all of which are in strong trade areas and share the potential of being a strong location.

Chapter 1

Identifying Areas With The Most Profit Potential For Your Wild Bird Store

This chapter describes how to begin your search for a location by narrowing down the world of possibilities to a more manageable area. While this book focuses on broad areas, its basic ideas can be applied to any area, with additional consideration given to differing consumer preferences and patterns.

The first question to answer is where you should look to build your new store. You probably have an area already in mind which is convenient to your office or home. If you have taken this approach then read this chapter with the intent of insuring that the market you have targeted has no significant negative characteristics.

By the end of this chapter you should have the tools to select several areas to prioritize.

The first step in identifying a location is to decide on a geographic area that is best suited for your concept. Typically the geographic location will be an area in a city or a county. You should typically identify two or three locations to work with.

Breaking down into prioritized areas that best support your wild bird store will require that you ask the three following questions:

1. Who is my consumer?

2. What demographic and consumer characteristic data is available?

3. Where are there matches between my consumer (demographics and characteristics) and the population within locations in my area of interest?

The remainder of this chapter will discuss how to answer these questions so that you can ultimately identify the most profitable territory for your business concept.

Who is my consumer?

Understanding your consumer is a crucial element for the success of your wild bird store. There are a couple of ways to learn about your consumer. You should analyze the current customer base of this industry (Check with Wild Bird Feeding Industry - see Appendix A) . Look at the demographics that surround your store potential location. (A 1 mile and 3 mile radius of population should give you a good set to learn from). Look at demographic information like population densities, daytime population densities, income levels, age, homeowners vs. renters and ethnicity. Then compare what you consider to be successful stores and their surrounding demographics with those stores that are not as successful and their associated demographics. Often there will be a correlation between certain demographic criteria and sales for the stores that do the best.

For example, you may find that anytime the median age of people within a 3 mile radius of your store is lower than 35 that sales slump. This would imply that your wild bird store may be sensitive to age and that targeting a older population would be more profitable. Or perhaps your wild bird store does not perform well when the median income drops below a certain level. As a result you will want to target areas where the income levels are higher. This process of comparing data associated with strong and weak sales is called regression analysis in statistics, and simply entails looking for parallels in data. Regression analysis is important and your should perform some form of this analysis and as a result have a very good "feel" for who your consumer is.

If your business is just starting out and examining an existing store base gives no conclusive answers? Then you should examine industry reports describing consumer trends, attitudes and behavioral patterns. Again go to Wild Bird Feeding Industry or US Fish and Wildlife Service for specific industry information on the wild bird business.

Where Does Your Consumer Live?

Whether your consumer is rich or poor, old or young, white collar or blue collar, married or single, or male or female, you are going to find them just about everywhere. What you need to do is first identify an area strong in the characteristics that comprise your consumer. Then you can proceed to the next important step of location analysis - identifying trade areas (Chapters 2 & 3).

Chapter 2

Trade Areas - What are they?

Introduction

In this chapter you will learn the meaning of the term "Trade Area" and gain a full understanding of the primary elements that make up a trade area. Each element is described, and a method is provided to help you analyze the strengths and weaknesses of each one.

A trade area is defined as a concentration of businesses where consumers go to exchange money for a variety of goods. Trade areas are best identified by the shopping centers or other population "draws" that act as their nucleus, but are in fact comprised of a number of different elements. The primary elements that make up a trade area are generators, traffic patterns, road configurations, demographics, day parts, seasonality and character. Understanding each of these elements and their strengths and weaknesses will allow you to identify, analyze, and evaluate effectively, the trade areas in your territory of analysis.

Trade area identification and analysis is an integral part of finding the right location. It allows you to break down a large territory identified in the previous chapter into smaller more manageable concentrations of activity. Trade areas can vary greatly in size often times from a half a block to a few miles. The size of the trade area is not as important as the elements that make it up, and how these elements compare to others in surrounding trade areas.

The following paragraphs define the elements of a trade area, explain why they are important, and show how to analyze them.

Generators

Generators are defined as anything that attracts people to a location. Some of the most common generators are shopping centers, grocery stores, malls, mass merchandisers, universities, theaters, stadiums and amusement parks. The generators in a trade area must be carefully evaluated since they are one of the primary elements that determine a trade area's strength or weakness. The success of a generator is measured by the number of people that come into the trade area because of it, and can be evaluated through observation. In addition, the time of the day and the days of the week that the generator attracts people should also be noted.

Generators are classified by their drawing power and fall into the following categories:

- International draw - example: Disneyland
- Regional draw - 30 mile radius of customer reach - example: Malls, Power Centers
- Multi-Neighborhood draw - 5 - 15 mile radius - examples include mass merchandisers.
- Neighborhood draw - 3 - 7 mile radius - examples include Grocery store shopping centers and basic retail oriented towards daily needs i.e. dry cleaners, video, shoe repair

Estimating the number of people that a generator attracts depends on the generator type, and can often be done on your own with a degree of accuracy sufficient for trade area analysis. The following are techniques for estimating a generator's strength: Amusement park attendance can be obtained through park officials, the city, or newspaper articles. A mall's success is best determined by comparing it to surrounding malls.

Ask yourself the following questions:

- Are there many cars in the parking lots?
- How many department stores does it have?
- Does the mall appear vibrant when you visit it?
- Mass merchandisers and grocery stores are best evaluated by comparing them to their nearby competition.
- What is the size of the parking lot? Does it fill up? How many cars are there?
- Are there numerous vacancies in the center?

A final way of gathering information about generators is to ask questions of people working in them. You can easily find out when a generator is busy and when it is slow. You can even find out which generator is the strongest in the area. For example, suppose you are in a KMart and ask the clerk, "How is that new Walmart down the street doing?" The clerk responds, "Ever since it opened we have not been busy. We used to have many people shopping in here on Saturdays and Sundays. It is much quieter now." From the clerk's response you learn that the number of people visiting KMart has declined and it appears to have affected weekend business.

Traffic Patterns & Character

Understanding the traffic patterns within a trade area will help you answer important questions, like what side of the street your business should be located. For example, suppose the major road running through a trade area is a commuter route for those headed to an office park 2 miles away. If you were selling coffee and donuts you will want to locate on the going-to-work side of the street. However you are a wild bird store so you would want to locate it on the going-home side of the street and stay open until the going home traffic subsided.

Traffic is characterized by the following terms:

- Through traffic - Cars pass by on their way to some destination outside the area.
- Commuter traffic - Similar to through traffic, but has the added characteristic of rush hour times in the morning and evening.

- Retail traffic - This traffic is largely due to the retail in the trade area. An example of this is a mall and the traffic it generates.
- Local traffic - This is traffic that primarily comes from nearby neighborhoods. This type of traffic usually occurs at small neighborhood shopping centers that are surrounded by homes.

The best ways to understand traffic and its patterns is by observation at different times of day, and through discussions with people in the trade area. Many retailers will be able to tell you, for example, that "at 5:30 p.m. there is traffic headed eastbound but the delay is only minor." Or, that "the intersection of First and Grand is very difficult during rush hours and should be avoided if possible."

Road Configurations

Road configurations are important to a trade area because they dictate how traffic moves through the area. Nearly everyone has experienced areas where traffic flow is terrible and making turns into shopping centers is very difficult. At the same time we have all experienced areas where road configurations help heavy traffic flow easily.

Familiarize yourself with the following road configurations and signs so that when you are analyzing trade areas, you will be able to identify key road configurations.

- Medians (see figure 2.1)
- Center turn lanes (see figure 2.2)
- Dedicated left turn lanes (see figure 2.3)
- Dedicated left turn lanes with protected signal (see figure 2.4)
- Dedicated right turn lanes (see figure 2.5)
- Primary and Secondary Streets (see figure 2.6)
- No left turn and no U-turn signs

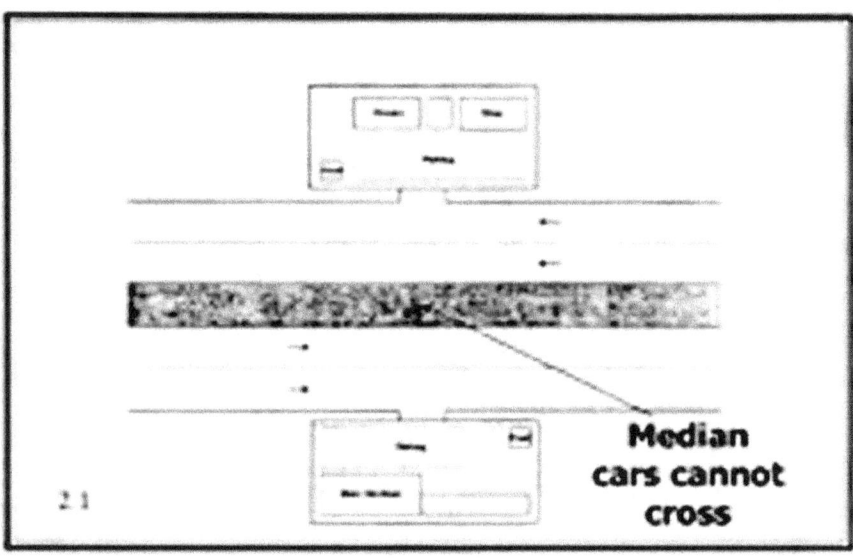

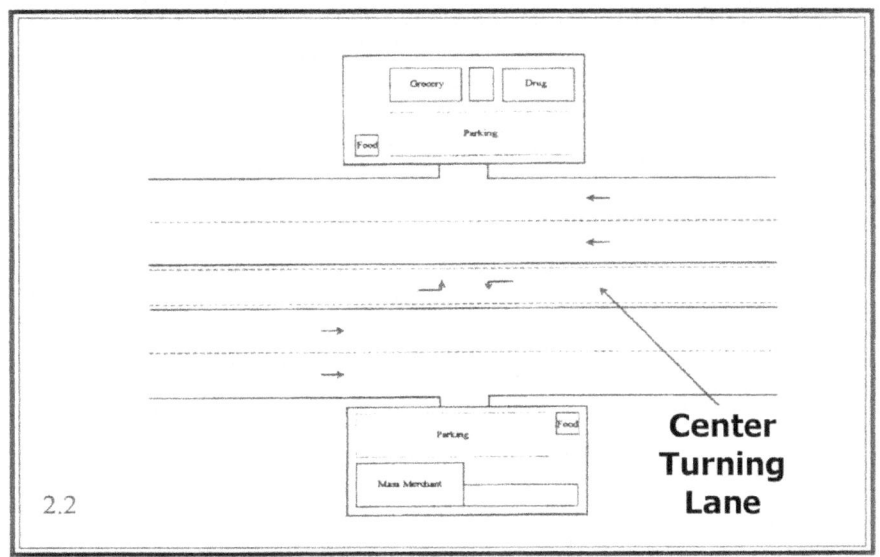

2.2

Center Turning Lane

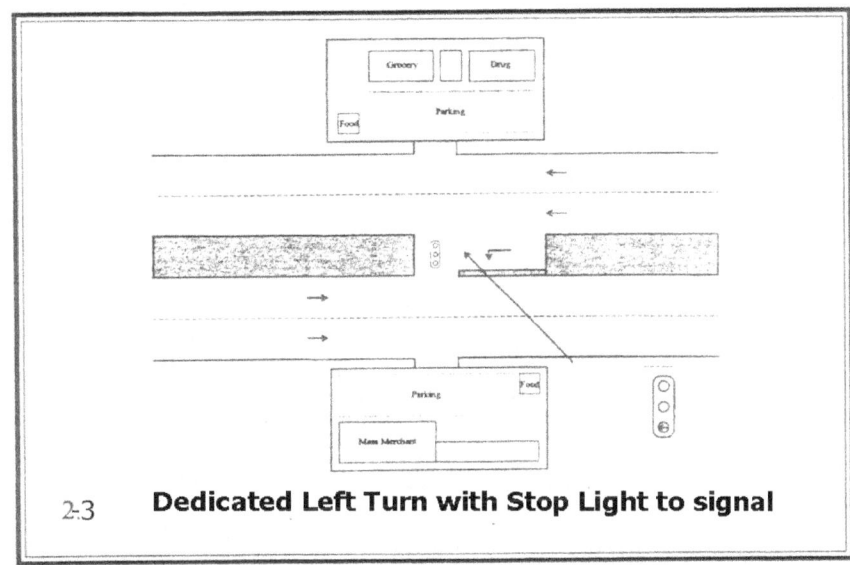

2-3 **Dedicated Left Turn with Stop Light to signal**

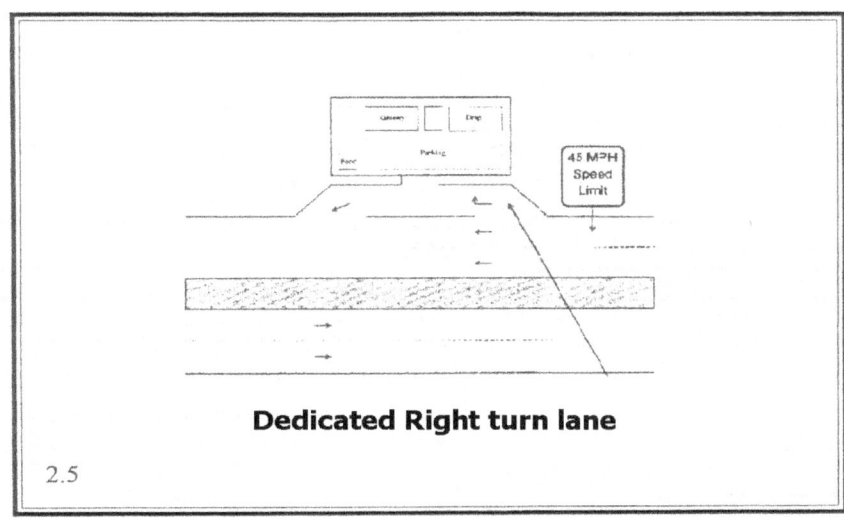

Dedicated Right turn lane

2.5

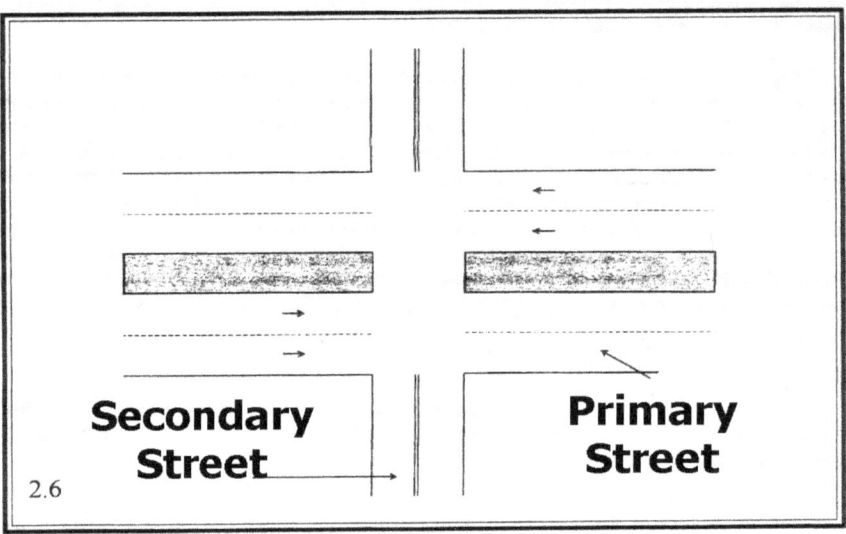

Demographics

The demographics of a trade area reveal not only the type of people that live in and around the area, but also the density of a given population. Demographic reports come in a variety of forms and can be obtained from numerous sources *(see Appendix A)*. Basic demographic information to obtain is:

- Population densities
- Population growth
- Daytime population densities (workers)
- Average household income (of those living in the trade area, not working in the trade area)
- Average age (of those living in the area)

Most demographic reports will include many additional variables such as types of businesses, population by race, households with children and education levels. But unless you understand that a correlation exists between these variables and your business it is difficult to determine whether the information is a positive or negative indication of the area.

See sample Demographic Report *(next page)*

Population density should be used as a minimum benchmark and those areas with numbers that are below these should be cautiously considered. Be sure that if a university or military base is in the area that you understand whether the population numbers are included in the totals or not. Also be aware of jails or penitentiaries. If the inmates are included in the population statistics then you most likely will want to subtract them out to better understand the true number of people who are able to visit your retail location.

Population stability or better yet growth is always desirable. Figures representing stable and growing numbers should be sought out. Be cautious of negative growth numbers within a 1 and 3 mile radius. To further understand growth in a trade area simply look around for signs of any new projects (either residential or retail) under construction. Also be sure to understand whether any

```
                POP-FACTS: FULL DATA REPORT
              (CENSUS '90, UPDATES & PROJECTIONS)


                  SAMPLE FULL DATA REPORT
ANY TWO CROSS STREETS
UNITED STATES OF AMERICA
```

DESCRIPTION	1.0 MILE RADIUS	3.0 MILE RADIUS	5.0 MILE RADIUS
POPULATION			
1999 PROJECTION	37184	88286	147737
1994 ESTIMATE	33475	79632	133011
1990 CENSUS	30943	73398	121368
1980 CENSUS	18573	43275	65480
GROWTH 1980 - 1990	66.60%	69.61%	85.35%
HOUSEHOLDS			
1999 PROJECTION	12869	30531	50964
1994 ESTIMATE	11333	28830	44487
1990 CENSUS	10215	24109	39658
1980 CENSUS	5804	13384	20050
GROWTH 1980 - 1990	76.00%	80.41%	97.80%
1994 ESTIMATED POPULATION BY RACE	33475	79632	133011
WHITE	62.42%	64.21%	69.34%
BLACK	4.34%	4.00%	3.83%
ASIAN & PACIFIC ISLANDER	29.80%	28.59%	23.98%
OTHER RACES	3.44%	3.21%	3.04%
1994 ESTIMATED POPULATION	33475	79632	133011
HISPANIC ORIGIN	12.00%	11.73%	11.40%
OCCUPIED UNITS	10215	24109	39658
OWNER OCCUPIED	57.90%	63.14%	64.63%
RENTER OCCUPIED	42.10%	38.86%	35.37%
1990 PERSONS PER HOUSEHOLD	3.03	3.01	2.97
1994 ESTIMATED HOUSEHOLDS BY INCOME	11333	28830	44487
$150,000 +	1.16%	2.02%	3.48%
$100,000 TO $149,999	4.42%	5.47%	7.31%
$ 75,000 TO $ 99,999	8.27%	11.14%	13.28%
$ 50,000 TO $ 74,999	30.61%	30.40%	28.45%
$ 35,000 TO $ 49,999	24.22%	22.54%	20.28%
$ 25,000 TO $ 34,999	15.29%	13.55%	12.04%
$ 15,000 TO $ 24,999	9.21%	8.25%	7.96%
$ 5,000 TO $ 14,999	4.70%	4.50%	5.06%
UNDER $5,000	2.13%	2.13%	2.11%
1994 ESTIMATED AVERAGE HH INCOME	$51,744	$55,927	$60,788
1994 ESTIMATED MEDIAN HH INCOME	$47,099	$50,338	$53,908
1994 ESTIMATED PER CAPITA INCOME	$17,525	$19,011	$20,736

significant sized companies are moving out of or into the area (you can get this information from the chamber of commerce or city officials as discussed in detail in the next chapter).

Daytime population figures are important because they will drive your lunch business. Those areas with very low daytime population levels are probably suburban, where people leave during the day for work and return at night. These areas will do most of their business during the weekday evenings and on the weekends. On the other hand, those areas with high daytime population figures are most likely urban in nature and will boast strong daytime business. Urban areas will vary with regards to strong evening and weekend business. This, however, is fairly easy to learn simply by observing the area during these times. *(See Day parts - next section)*

Income:

While income numbers are important to a trade area and the success of a concept, those income levels that are optimal will range depending on your business concept. It is useful to compare this data with the demographic data from other trade areas to become comfortable with the variances in demographics within the territory you have chosen to analyze.

Age:

Finally, the average age range of 25 - 40 is a fairly normal range. Areas with numbers falling outside of this range, lets assume on the high side, will indicate that the area may be a retirement community. This may be good because your wild bird business caters to the elderly. However in all cases, you should exercise caution in considering this area or any area for your store.

Keep in mind that you can get a feel for basic demographic criteria in general terms simply by looking around. Population, growth, daytime population, income and age can all be estimated with a general degree of accuracy when driving through an area. This will allow you to determine quickly whether the trade area you are studying will support your wild bird store or not. While driving through a trade area you notice that most of the homes are not kept up, cars appear to be older models and surrounding businesses seem to cater to lower income families. You can probably conclude within ten minutes of driving the area that the income levels of this area are too low for your a wild bird speciality store. Even if you find the prime site in this trade area you should most likely not pursue it. Basic trade area elements must be strong and support your concept. Remember, NO site within a poor trade area is a good location.

Day parts

Day parts, simply defined, are those parts of the day that a trade area is vibrant. Understanding the day parts of a trade area and how they relate to your business concept will allow you to fully realize the sales potential of your store. An example is a sandwich shop in an area where the daytime population is strong. This unit would thrive off the lunch business created through employees. Typically day parts are classified by the following groups:

Weekday	**Weekend**
Breakfast	Breakfast
Lunch	Lunch
Dinner	Dinner

Those trade areas that are vibrant during numerous day parts are most attractive for achieving strong sales performances. Aligning the strong day parts of a trade area with your wild bird store needs will be a crucial part of your business's ability to reach its maximum sales potential.

Seasonality

Seasonality is the change in vibrancy in a trade area during periods of a year. An example is a ski resort town which is vibrant during winter months and slower during summer months. Another example is a small college town which is vibrant throughout most of the year except the summer months when the students are on break. Identifying these changes in vibrancy is crucial to properly evaluating a trade area and usually can be accomplished by talking with the chamber of commerce and city.

Chapter 3

Identifying, Analyzing & Prioritizing Trade Areas - How You Do It

This chapter describes how to identify, evaluate, and prioritize trade areas. The first step of the process is to collect information like maps, demographic reports, street finders, etc. to familiarize yourself generally with the area you have selected through the process described in Chapter 1. Once you have collected this information, the next step will be to gather additional information, following the process outlined here, from within the trade area itself. Finally, after you have generated enough information, the last step will be to organize and evaluate it, so that you can then compare one trade area to another.

MAPS

The first step in identifying trade areas is to get maps of the territory you are looking at (as identified per chapter 1). Convenience stores and book stores sell maps. The chamber of commerce and city offices usually have maps as well.

Insure that the maps you get are highly detailed and are not general overview maps. In addition, make sure that the maps cover the entire territory you are researching. Always get three or four copies of each map. The first couple will be used as a working copies and the remaining will be used for your final plan.

Consider using a street finder from Thomas Brothers or Rand McNally - two of the larger map book producers. Probably available at the Library. These highly detailed maps can be very useful since they often show shopping centers, malls, universities, and other important real estate developments important for your research.

See Figure 3.1 (next page)

Legend Of Map Symbols

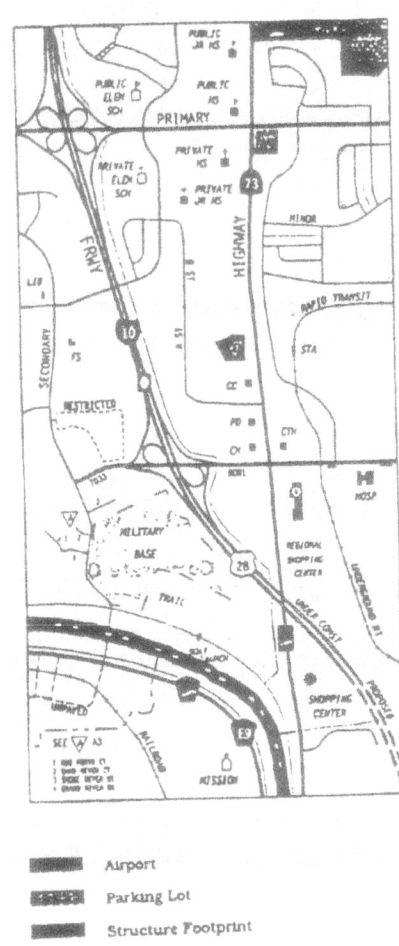

	Airport
	Parking Lot
	Structure Footprint
	Regional Shopping Center
	Major Dept. Store (List of Abbr. page)

	Freeway
	Interchange / Ramp
	Highway
	Primary Road
	Secondary Road
	Minor Road
	Restricted Road
	Alley
	Dirt Road
	Proposed Road. Under Const.
	Proposed Freeway
	Freeway Under Construction
	One-Way Road
	Two-Way Road

5	Interstate
5	Interstate (Business)
3	U.S. Highway
1	State Highway
2	County Highway
	State Scenic Highway
	County Scenic Highway
	Carpool Lane
	Street List Marker
	Street Continuation
	Street Termination
✈	Airport
	Station (Train, Bus, Ranger)
	Building (see List of Abbreviations page)
	Building Footprint
	Public Elementary School
	Public High School
	Private Elementary School
	Private High School
	Shopping Center

3.1

Carefully study the legends of your maps and street finders so that you understand the symbols and color codes used. This information is extremely valuable in helping you identify potential trade areas. While this step is easy to brush over, you should take the time to completely understand the legends of your maps.

Study your maps

After getting maps spend some time at home or the office (not in your car) carefully studying them. First review the legends and learn the symbols and color codes used (as discussed above). Most people discover at this stage that a map shows much more than initially meets the eye. Become comfortable with the symbols and codes used and what they mean. Be sure to study an area that is large enough to produce numerous potential trade areas for your study. This will probably range from five to ten square miles. Then attempt to answer the following questions:

- How does the freeway system service the area?
- Where are the main commuting thoroughfares? Are they obvious from the map, or will you need to drive them to make sure?
- Where do people work?
- Where do people live?
- Where are the malls and other major shopping centers (i.e. generators)?
- Are there rivers, lakes, railroads or mountains that effect traffic flow throughout the area?

Visit the Chamber of Commerce

Most cities have a chamber of commerce which is formed to promote the city to businesses and the general public. They provide information about the city (usually free of charge) to the public. You should visit the Chamber of Commerce (COC) and ask for the following:

¨   City demographics - this will give you statistics on population, growth, age, race, education level, income, etc.

- Major Employers - this is usually a list of the largest employers in the city that includes the type of business and the number of employees each has.
- New Developments - Sometimes the Chamber of Commerce will provide information regarding new developments in the city (i.e. the construction of a new mall). This question should also be asked of the city (next section).
- Economic Reports - Sometimes the COC in conjunction with the city will provide research reports which are intended to give the public information on the economic climate of the city. The reports can range from a couple pages to a sophisticated compilation of research regarding the area and its economic, demographic, real estate and business environment.

Visit the City and the Department of Transportation (DOT)

Next visit the city hall (general information or planning department) and ask them if the following is available:

- General Plan - this will reveal the city's plans for managing future growth through the zoning or specified use of available land. The plan will help you develop a general idea of where homes, office and industrial parks, and shopping centers are located. Be sure to ask if there are any new large residential projects and where the city is projected to have the most growth.
- Demographic Reports, Economic Reports and Real Estate Reports - These are the reports, discussed in the previous section, that fall under many different titles and provide valuable information on the city's current statistics.
- Special Permits for your use - Discuss the nature of your business to learn about any special permits you may need.

At the Department of Transportation ask for:

Traffic count maps - these maps will give you statistics on the number of cars traveling on streets throughout the city. Insure that you understand how the numbers are defined. Are the daily counts for both sides of the street or for one direction only? Either format of counts will work. You will use this map to analyze the vibrancy of an identified trade area as well an identified site.

Road Changes - Ask the DOT if there are any new roads planned, where they are, what the status of the plans are and the completion date. In addition ask about any significant changes to current roads. This information is crucial to understand because a road change can significantly change traffic patterns and counts in a trade area. There is nothing quite like having the road in front of your store closed for repairs over a six months period. Ask !!

Identify Trade Areas

Once you have obtained and studied maps, met with the city, DOT and COC, the next step is to identify and visit trade areas. There are two ways to go about this and they depend on the type of information you were able to gather.

The first method is to locate all major retail developments on your map within the geographic territory you are covering and then to go and visit these areas. It depends on having obtained data that specifies where retail developments are located.

The second method is to get in your car and drive the major streets within the territory in search of major retail developments. While this method is more time consuming, you will become very familiar with your territory through the exercise. Most of the large retail companies use this method as it is more thorough.

You should aim for identifying between 3 and 5 trade areas for your wild bird store. Later, the trade areas will be ranked and specific sites within them will be pursued. Some areas may rank very low, so sites within them will not be sought out. Other trade areas will rank high and will be revisited to identify potential sites (chapter 4). The idea is to have enough trade areas so that you can rank them, select the top trade areas, and pursue specific sites - one of which will ultimately be the best site for your concept.

Analyze The Trade Area

When you enter a trade area there is a sequence of steps you should follow to evaluate and understand its elements fully. The following set of steps, along with the check list and trade area form will guide you through the process.

Step 1 - Drive the entire area and become familiar with where the trade area begins and ends.

Usually the beginning or ending will be apparent through the change from retail concentrations to residential concentrations. Other times retail developments may extend for miles. In this situation look for demographic changes between higher and lower income levels, or real estate changes like newer developments as compared to mature ones. Do not become overly concerned with the boundaries of the trade areas. Focus instead on the elements and character of the area.

Step 2 - Draw a map on a sheet of paper.

Start by drawing the primary road in the area. Then drive to one end of the trade area and as you drive back through the trade area note the locations of the following on your map:

- Generators
- Competitors
- National players
- Major cross streets

Because driving and writing at the same time is difficult, you should drive through the trade area looking only at the items on the right side of the street. Stay in the right lane and pull over into parking lots frequently to note what you saw. Continue this process until you reach the end of the trade area then turn around and drive back taking note of the other side of the street.

While this process sounds time consuming it will provide you all the information you need to properly evaluate (and recall) the trade area.

Step 3 - Fill out the Trade Area Form *(Appendix B.)*.

Note that to complete the form you will need to drive the trade area again looking for additional information.

After step 3 you should have a completed hand drawn map and a form for this trade area. These two sheets should then be stapled together and filed. To insure that all the essential steps have been completed, quickly review the check list (Appendix C). If you were unable to obtain any of the information make a note on the check list and include the list in your file as a follow up reminder.

Repeat the above process for each of the trade areas in your area of study.

Prioritizing the Trade Areas

Review the trade areas you analyzed. Remember to look at the trade area as a whole with the intent of understanding its different elements. Avoid focusing on any specific site until the trade areas have been prioritized. Focus on the different elements as outlined in chapter 2 and look at their strengths and weaknesses. Then compare one trade to another and establish a method to designate the top ranking trade areas. Colored dots (available in office supple stores) are recommended as they serve as a good visual reference for the ranking of the trade areas. An example may be gold for those trade areas ranking highest, silver for the next level of trade areas etc. Once you have finished ranking the trade areas, proceed to chapter 4 where you will look for a specific site.

Chapter 4

Selecting a Site

This chapter will guide you through the process of selecting sites within the trade areas you have identified. First, a thorough description of the factors that contribute to a site's desirability is presented. After this, the process to find specific sites is described.

The Elements of a Site

A site's strength can vary greatly depending on its:

- Type
- Positioning in the trade area
- Visibility
- Access
- Parking
- Flow of traffic in the parking lot serving it
- Signage
- Size & Dimensions

All of the above elements are important to consider when looking for a site. Yet all the elements do not have to be exceptional for a site to be desirable. In fact there are very few sites that rank exceptionally high in all of the above elements. Most strong sites are exceptional in a couple of the elements and average to above average in the remaining elements. The key to keep in mind is to avoid sites that suffer from a few below average elements.

The following paragraphs describe these elements in detail.

Type

A site generally falls into one of two categories; freestanding and in-line. Freestanding sites are those where a building stands independently of other buildings. They typically have only one tenant and dedicated parking for the building. Many of the fast food restaurants you see such as McDonald's, Burger King and Taco Bell are freestanding. In-line sites, on the other hand, house multiple tenants side by side and thus each tenant shares a wall and parking with a neighboring tenant. Wild Bird Stores usually have in line sites. Both freestanding sites and In-line sites are further broken down as follows:

FREESTANDING

    Corner
    Mid block
    Pad

IN-LINE

    End Cap Corner
    In-Line Corner
    End Cap Mid block
    In-Line Mid block

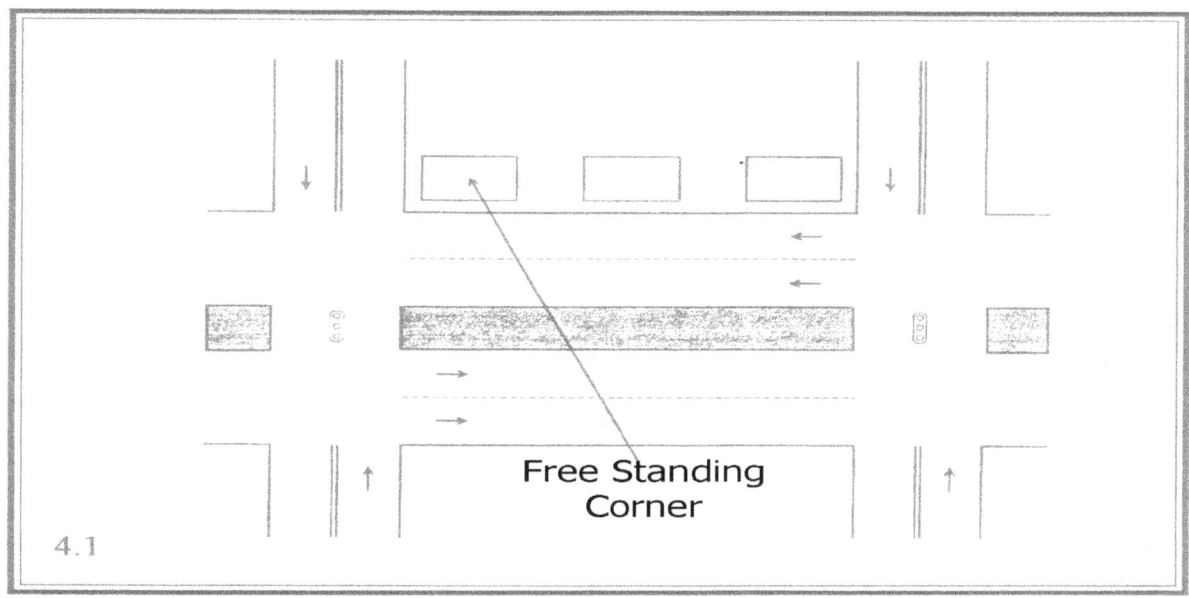

Free Standing Corner

4.1

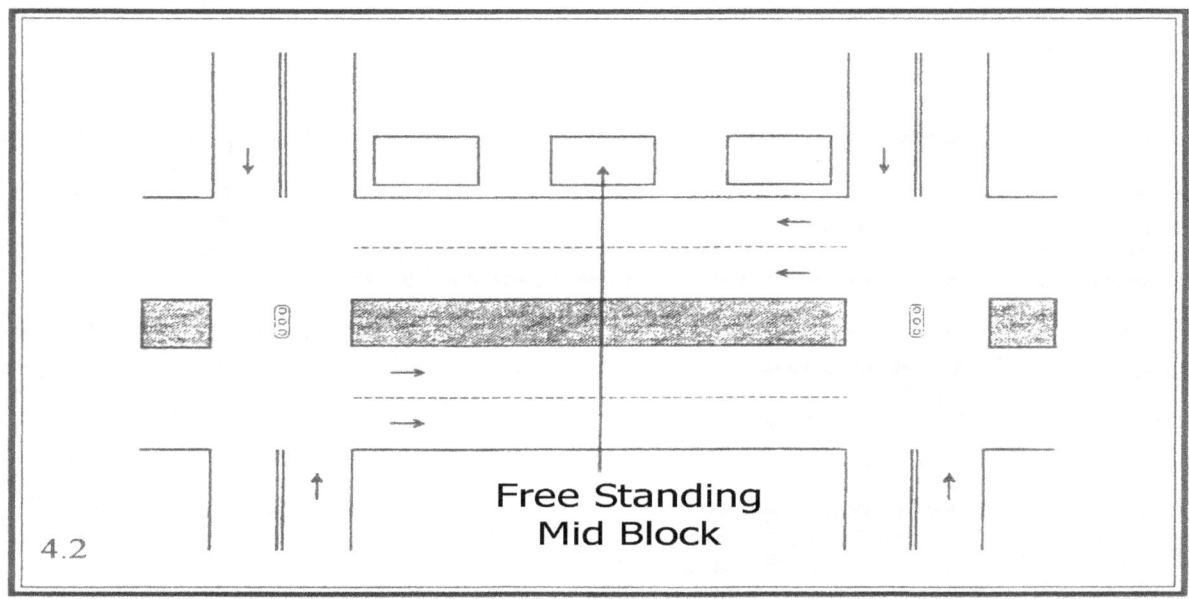

Free Standing Mid Block

4.2

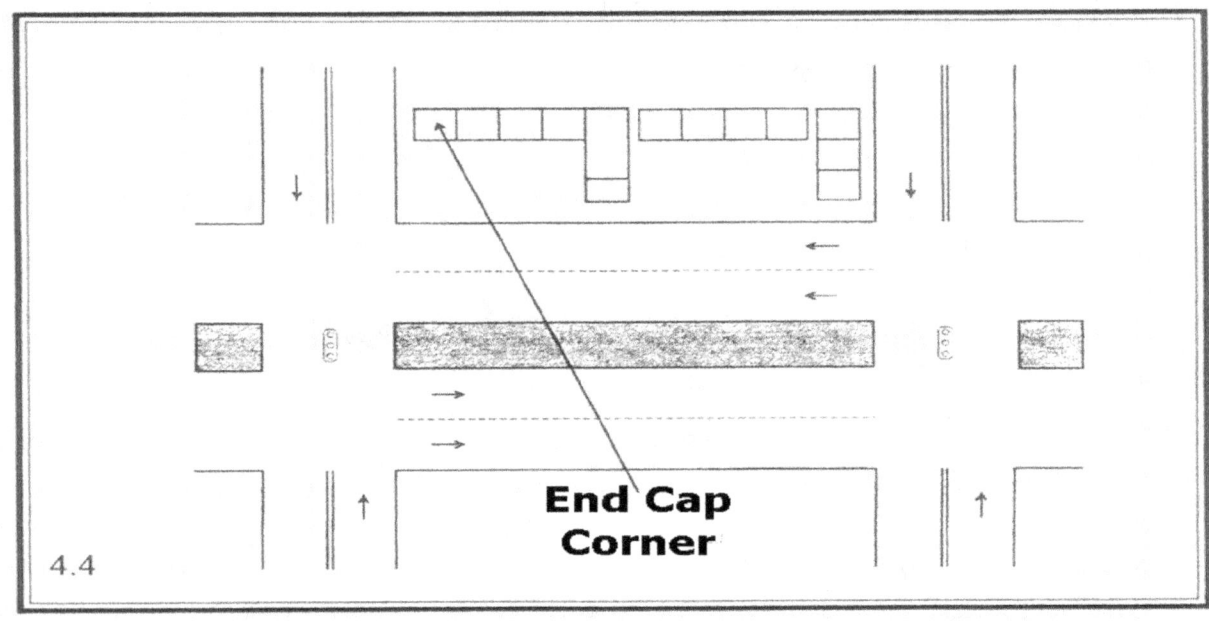

End Cap Corner

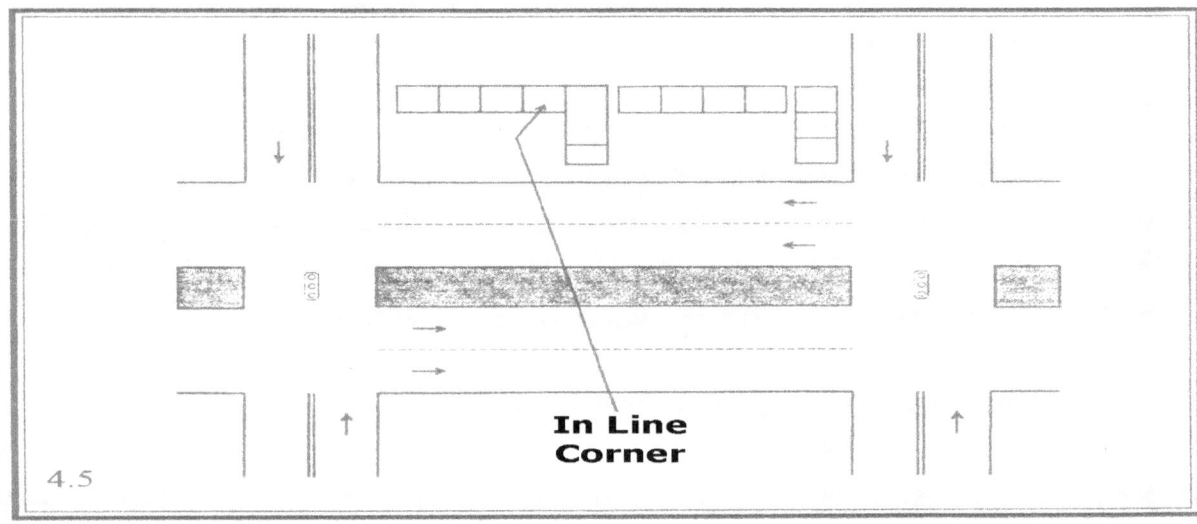

In Line Corner

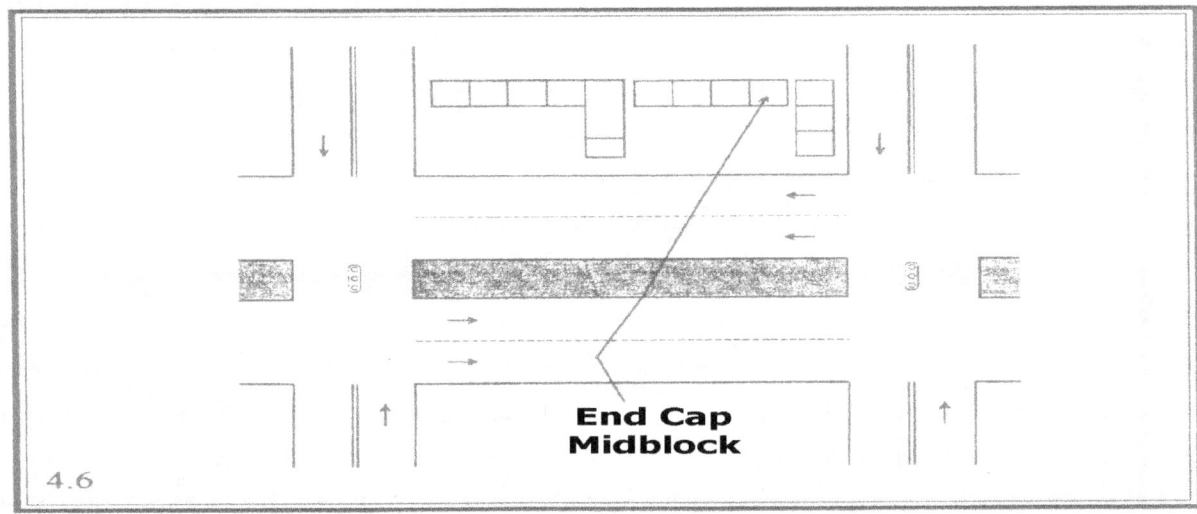

End Cap Midblock

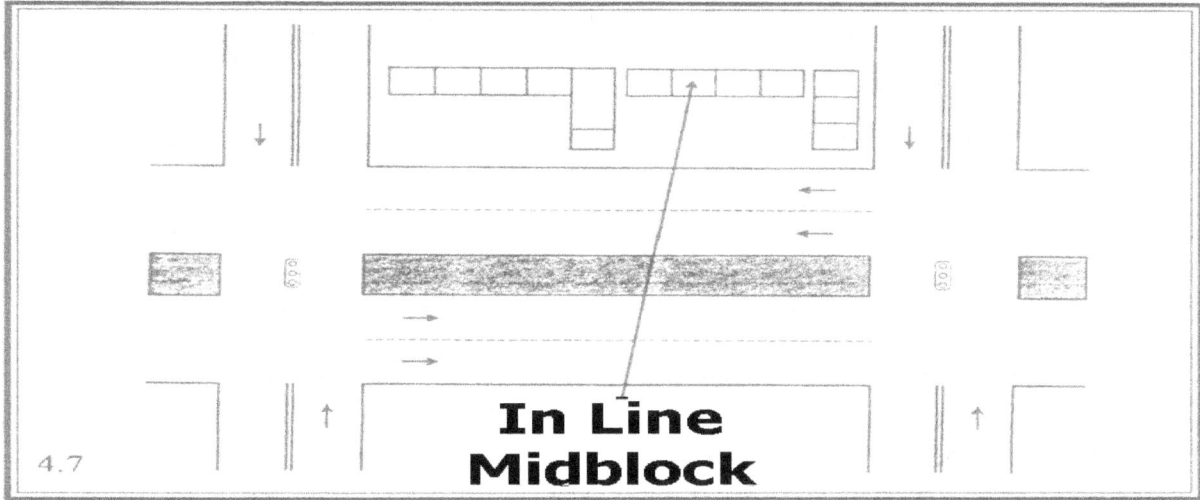

Positioning in the Trade Area

Because a trade area's vibrancy may fluctuate from one end to the other, it is important to choose a site that is positioned so that it can benefit from the most vibrant parts of the trade area. Identifying the strongest generators will highlight the vibrant parts of the trade area. Ask yourself the following questions about a site you are considering:

- Where is the site in the trade area?
- Is it in the middle of the most vibrant part?
- Is it near a generator?
- Is it near the strongest generator?
- Where is the competition?
- Do they have better positioning in the trade area with respect to the site you are considering?
- Is the trade area growing? In which direction?
- After growth occurs will your site still be in a highly vibrant part of trade area?

Visibility

The more visible your site is, the more chance you have at attracting impulse customers. Additionally, visibility will play an integral role in building consumer awareness for your product. For example if you have a site that is visible from a street that is a major thoroughfare from the freeway to homes then you will gain constant exposure to people driving by your site.

Ask yourself the following questions about your site's visibility:

- Is your site visible from the primary road in the trade area?
- Is the site visible from any other roads in the trade area?
- Is your site visible from the primary entrance into your site or shopping center?
- If the site is part of a generator, can it be seen by people going into and out of the major store?

- If your site is not part of a major generator can it be seen by people at a major generator nearby?
- How does the visibility of your site compare to the competition?

Access

The ability to easily access your site is absolutely crucial. Because convenience is so important to consumers, you must insure that the site you choose has exceptional access. Access is usually viewed in terms of ingress and egress, both of which are important. Ingress is the ability to get into the site from the road. Egress is the ability to exit the site. Often your site will be part of a shopping center and will share the entrances and exits that the center provides. In these cases, the access issues you should analyze are those of the shopping center. For sites that are not a part of a shopping center, you should simply analyze the access directly to and from the site. Look at each access point and ask yourself the following questions:

- Is this an ingress point? Egress point? Both?
- Can cars make a left turn into the site or shopping center?
- Can cars make a left turn out of the site or shopping center?
- Is it difficult to accomplish these left turns?
- Is there a center turn lane?
- Is there a dedicated left turn lane?
- Is there a left turn protected signal allowing cars to easily make left turns?
- Is there a median prohibiting convenient access to the center?
- Does traffic back up at a signal and thus block an entrance / exit to the site? (See Figure 4.8)
- Is one access point stronger than the others?
- Which access point is least functional?
- Which access point is least popular?
- Is the site or shopping center mid-block?
- Is the site or shopping center on a near or far corner? (See Figure 4.9)

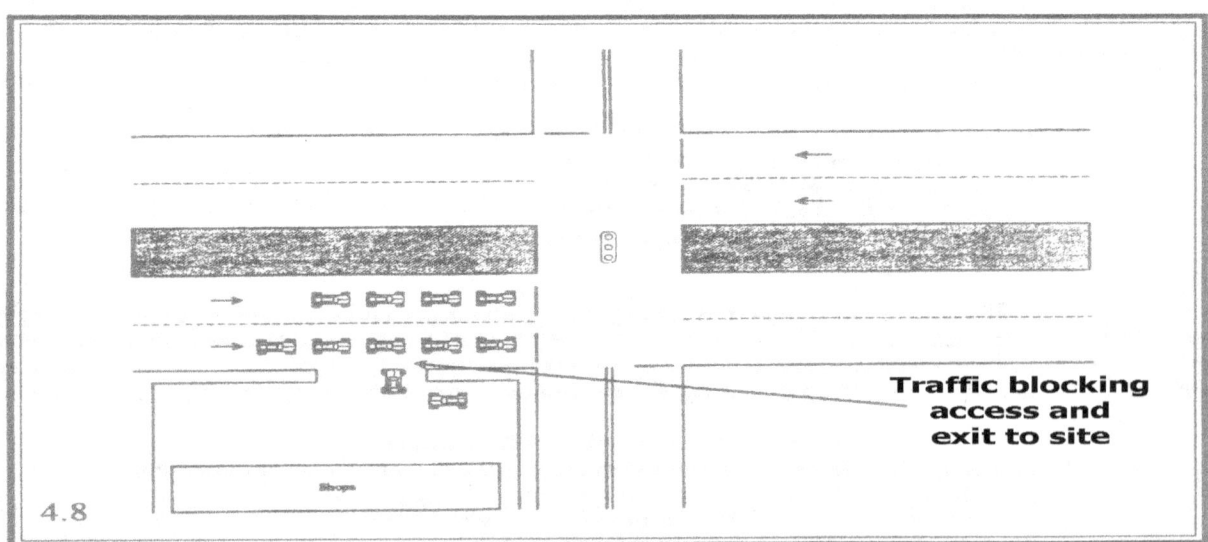

4.8

Traffic blocking access and exit to site

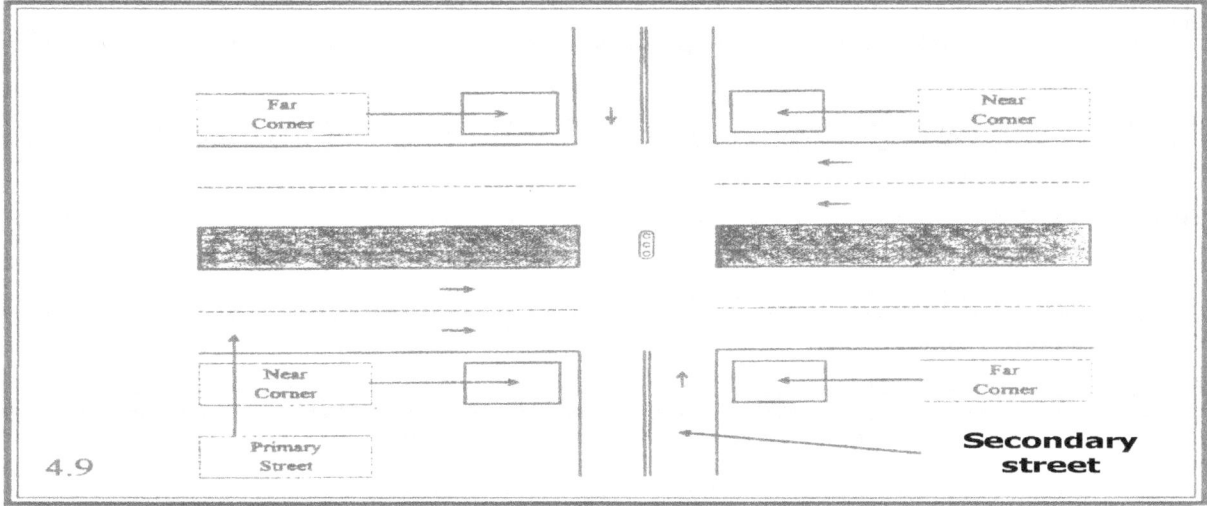

Parking

The number of parking spots that customers can conveniently use at the site is also crucial to a site's desirability. Be sure to examine the parking lot that services a site at different times of the day and on weekends as well as weekdays. Look out for neighboring tenants that produce a large number of cars for an extended period of time such as gyms and movie theaters. Ask yourself the following questions:

- Are there any times that the site lacks adequate parking?
- Do neighboring tenants have the same hours of operation as those of your store?
- Are there any neighbors that may cause a parking problem?
- How convenient are the parking spots to the actual store?
- How does the parking compare to that of the competition?
- How easy is it for your staff or customers to carry a 50 lb of bird seed to the car.

Flow

When a potential site is part of a shopping center, strip center or other generator (this is the case nearly all the time), you should observe the flow of traffic within the center's parking lot. Some centers handle traffic very well and consequently avoid grid lock during peak hours. Other centers unfortunately have poor layouts and therefore are more susceptible to traffic flow problems.

By observing the center during different times of the day and different days of the week, you will gain a good understanding of any flow problems that the center might have.

Signage

The importance of signage to the success of your business cannot be overemphasized. McDonald's is an expert in sign usage. Their signs are always very visible and often can be seen from multiple directions and from far enough away to allow customers to make an impulse decision and turn into the site. The success of McDonald's signs are an example that other industry players strive to emulate. The general philosophy is to obtain as big and as visible a sign as possible for your site.

Given that sign ordinances change from city to city <u>you will need to check with the city in which your site is located to determine what sign restrictions might exist.</u> By observing other tenants in your site's shopping center, you can get a good feel for the types of signs that are allowed as well as who has the most visible and readable signs.

Obtain answers to the following questions by talking with the city or landlord:

- Can you get your own pole sign? (See Figure 4.10)
- Can you share an existing pole sign that other tenants are currently using? (See Figure 4.11)
- Can you get a monument sign? (See Figure 4.12 & 4.13)
- Can you get a building sign? How many? (See Figure 4.14)
- Can you put signs in your windows? (See Figure 4.15)

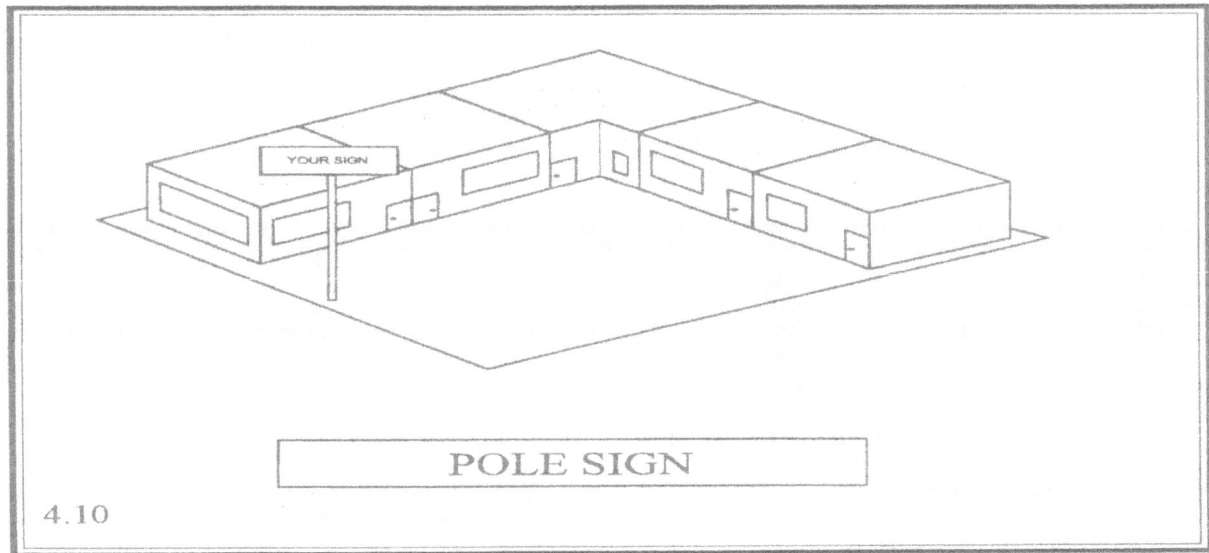

POLE SIGN

4.10

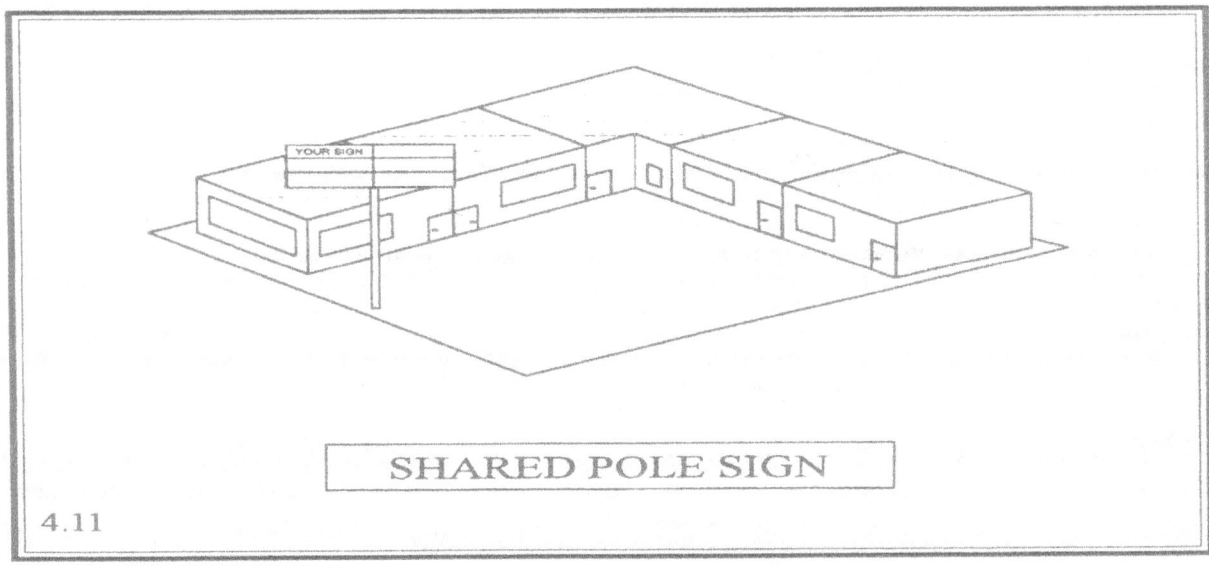

SHARED POLE SIGN

4.11

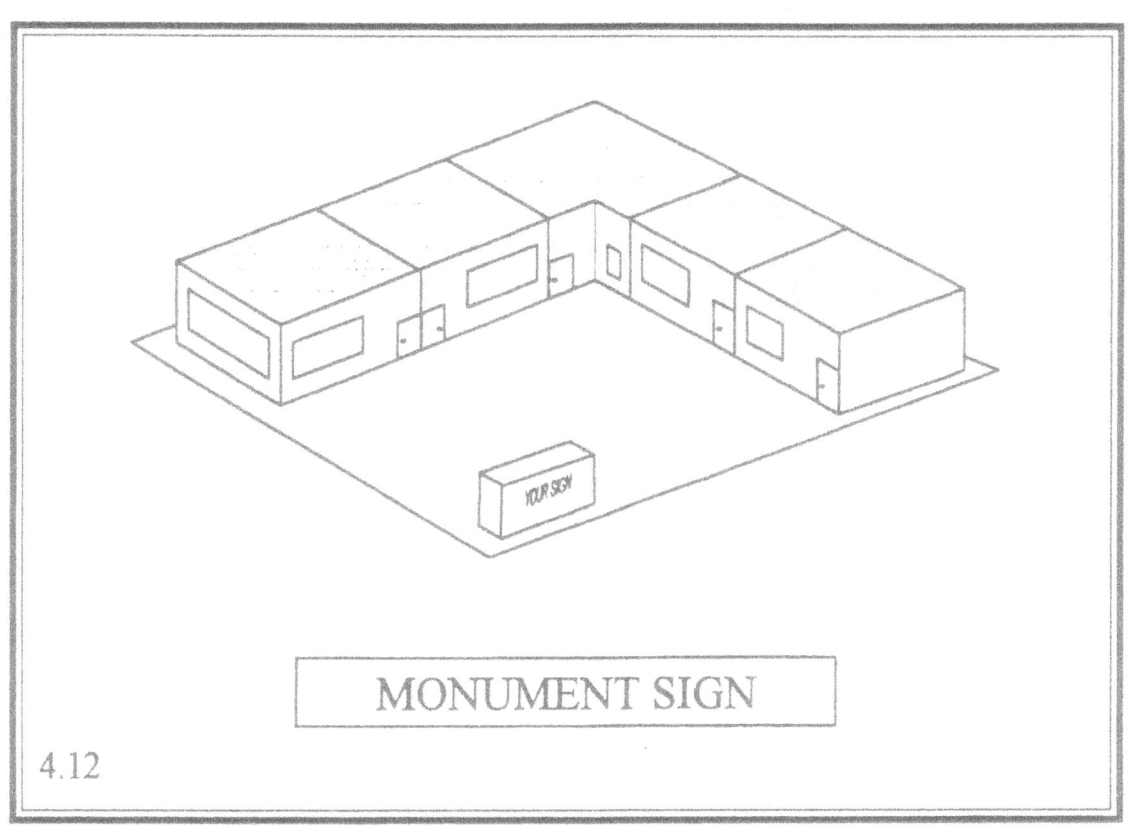

MONUMENT SIGN

4.12

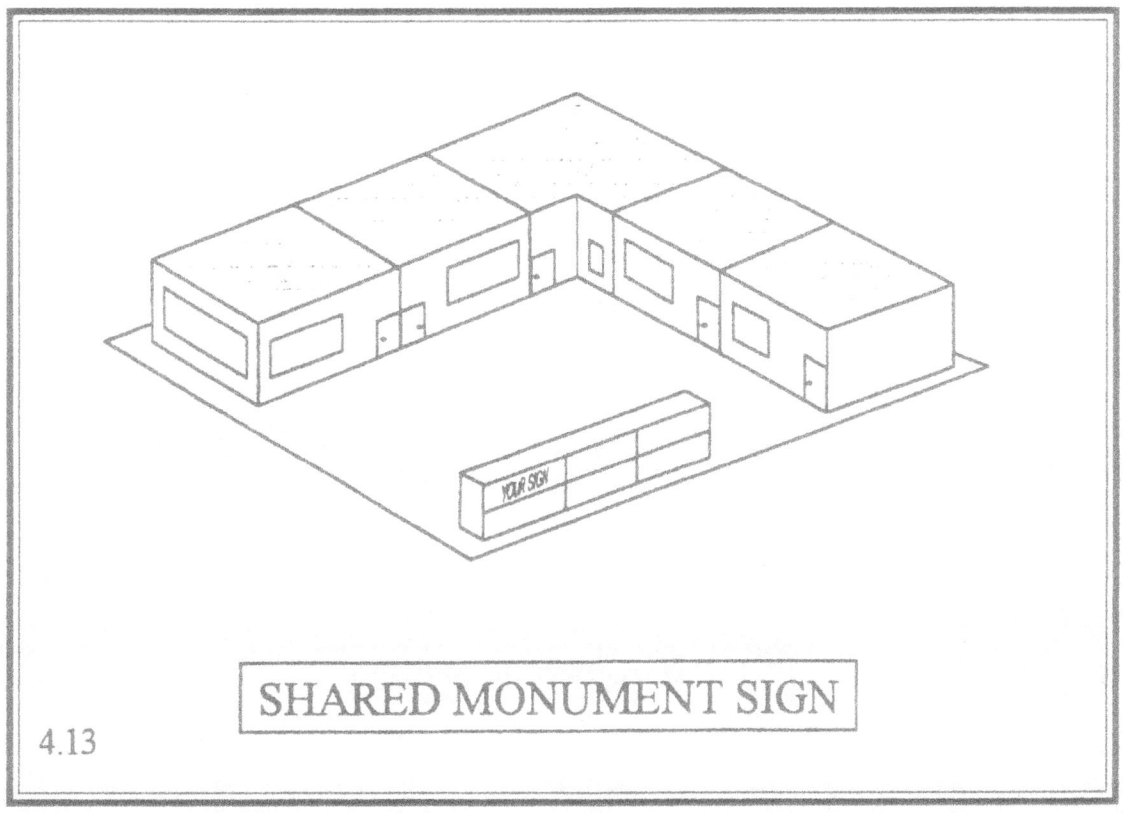

SHARED MONUMENT SIGN

4.13

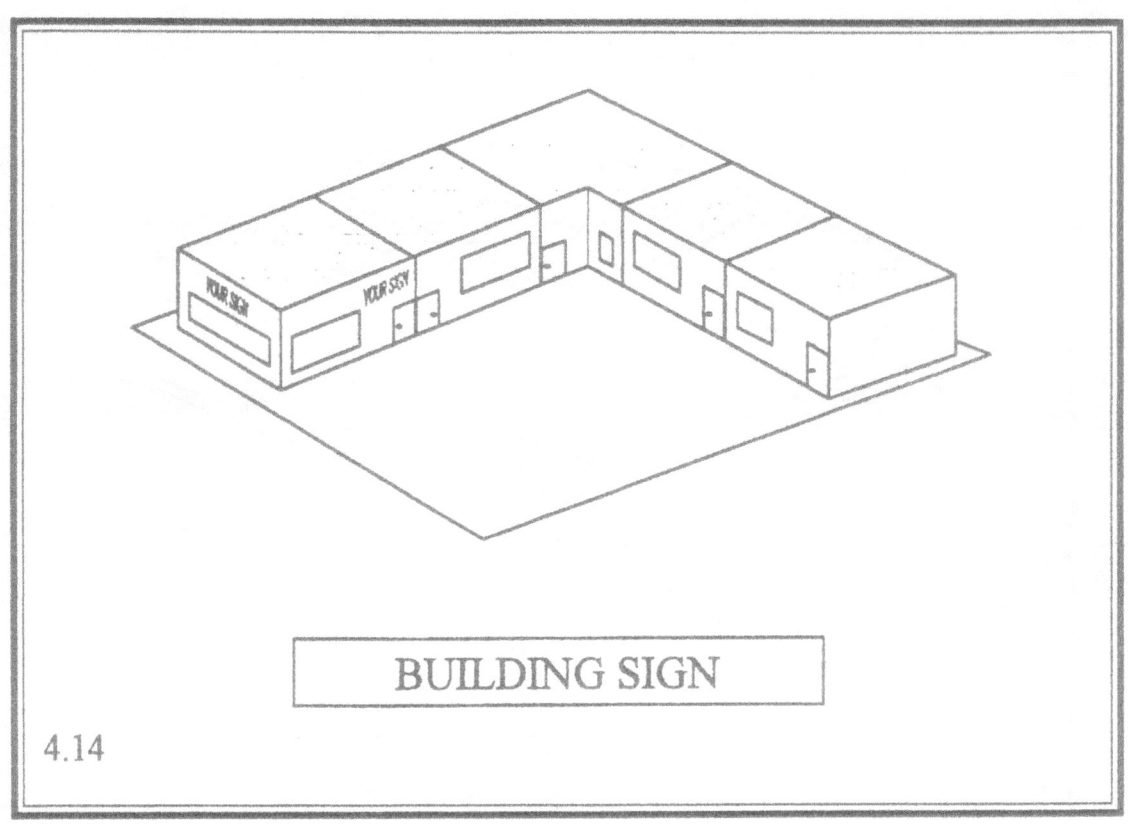

BUILDING SIGN

4.14

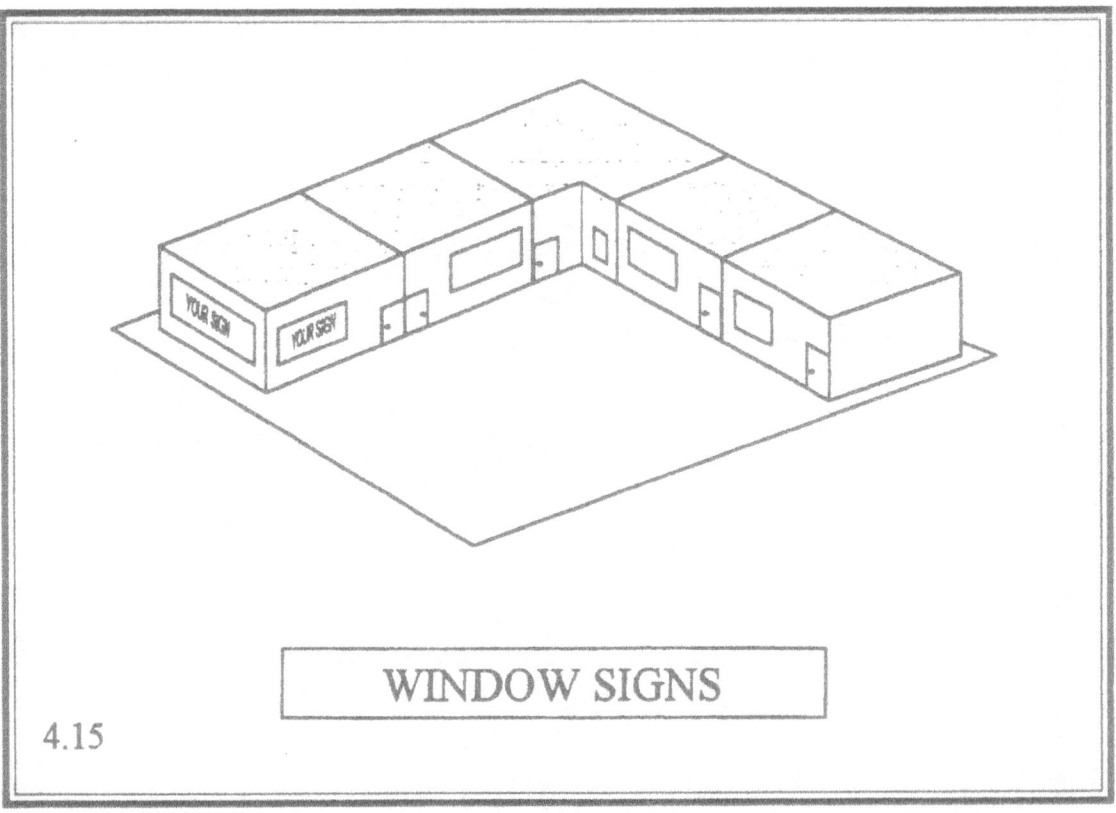

WINDOW SIGNS

4.15

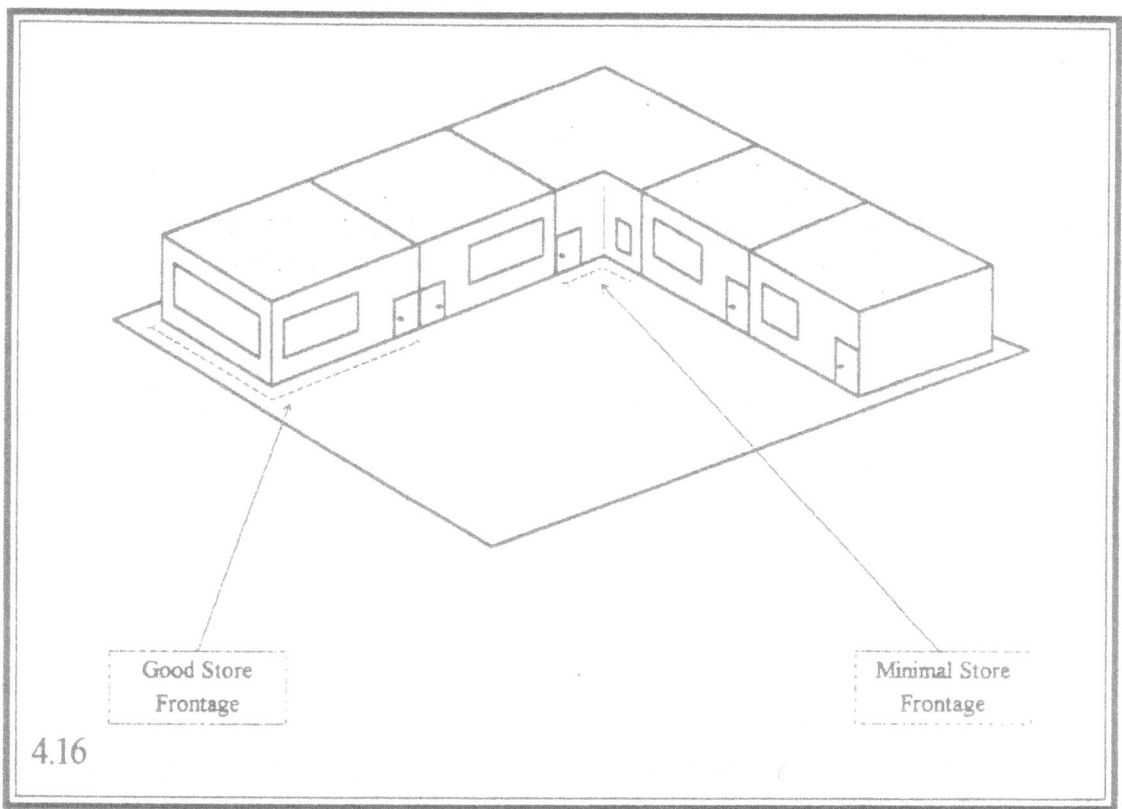

Good Store
Frontage

Minimal Store
Frontage

4.16

Size & Dimensions of site

The size and dimensions of the site you are considering should be close to what you have laid out for your store. Be sure that you have a good understanding of these requirements because too much or too little square footage, as well as irregular or awkward dimensions, can be a significant problem.

Here are some of the problems that can arise if your site has the wrong size and dimensions:

Too little square footage creates operational problems and induces artificial caps on sales for your business through the inability to service customers properly at peak times. Too much space means that you will be paying rent for unused square footage.

Sites with irregular or awkward dimensions can leave you with undesirable and unusable space. An example is a site in the shape of a long and skinny rectangle. The minimal width not only reduces your visibility to customers looking for your store front, but also creates an undesirable cavernous or "bowling alley" feeling.

Finding Sites

There are numerous ways to finding potential sites within the trade areas that you have identified. First drive to the trade area that tops your priority list as created in chapter 2. Then go to the most vibrant part of the trade area and begin looking for an available site (see method 1 below). In the event that there are no sites available there may still be an opportunity to find a site (as outlined in method 2). The key is to start in the very best area within the trade area and to work your way around this spot, designating any possible sites as priority sites. Next, move to the next best spot in the trade area and repeat the process. Hopefully you will be able to select a few potential sites that you can pursue. Keep in mind that sometimes there simply may be no sites available. In this case you can choose to consult with a broker who can search the area further for you (see method 3), or go to the next trade area on your priority list.

Method 1

The primary way to find a site is to call the contact (usually a broker who represents the landlord / owner) listed on a for lease or sale sign. During your initial discussion be sure to ask the following questions:

- How many square feet (sq.ft.) does the site have?
- What are its dimensions?
- When is it available for lease?
- Are there any restrictions on the use of the space that would prevent your concept?
- What is the asking rate for the space?
- Is this triple net?
- What are the average triple net expenses?
- What type of signage is available for the site?

Note that rent is almost always quoted on a per square foot basis. But sometimes (depending on where you are in the United States) it is annually and other times it is monthly. For example, the asking price might be $18 per sq. ft. per year. This would be equal to $1.50 / per sq. ft. / month. Once you become comfortable with market rates for your area you will know whether the rate quoted is yearly or monthly.

Method 2

The second method is used in the case of a center where no space appears to be available. In this situation, simply obtain the landlord's name, address and phone number from an existing tenant. Then call the landlord and identify yourself as a prospective tenant who is interested in any space that might become available through expiring leases or through existing tenants that are interested in subleasing, quitting their lease early, or giving up extra space.

While method 2 seems a harder way to find potential sites, many sites actually surface this way. The advantage is that you can learn about a possible site before it is advertised publicly.

Method 3

Method 3 is to consult a broker to aid in finding you a site in the desired area. Brokers are paid by the landlord or seller, so theoretically it will not cost you anything. We term it theoretically because use you may be able to negotiate a cheaper deal when a broker is not involved since their fee will not be a part of the deal.

Choosing an experienced and reputable broker is very important. Do some research before choosing one. Once you have chosen one, you must give them direction as to where (i.e. which trade areas) you want them to look for you. Be strict with the areas you have prioritized since brokers may want to show you sites that fall outside these areas.

Chapter 5

Negotiating the Lease

Now that you have identified a strong location and spoken with the landlord regarding its availability and size, it's time to negotiate a letter of intent and lease (or purchase agreement when you are purchasing a building or parcel of land).

A: The Letter of Intent: - The purpose of the letter of intent is to come to an agreement on the basic terms and conditions of the deal without getting bogged down in legal details. The basic terms and conditions commonly defined in a letter of intent are:

■ **Primary Term** - The initial number of years of the lease.

■ **Options to extend:** Outlines one or more options that give the lessee the power to extend the lease for a predetermined number of years. A typical example would be to have 2 options to extend the lease term for an additional 5 years each. These 2 options would effectively give you 10 more years to lease the space. One option would be exercised at the end of the primary term and the second would be exercised at the end of the first option.

■ **Rental Rate:** This is simply the agreed rent which is either stated in a monthly or annual figure.

■ **Type of Lease:** Leases of retail space are usually divided into two categories - Triple Net and Full Service Gross. The primary difference between the two is who (i.e. lessor or lessee) pays for certain expenses. A triple net lease means that the lessee is responsible for the expenses. A full service gross lease means that the landlord is responsible for the expenses. The specific expenses in question are taxes, insurance and maintenance (the triple in triple net). These are expenses for the center as a whole. Therefore under a triple net lease the lessee would be responsible for paying his or her share of the taxes, insurance and maintenance of the center. The share of expenses any lessee is responsible for is prorated in terms of the number of square feet they occupy. As an example, if you lease 2,000 sq. ft. from a center that has 100,000 sq. ft. of feasible space, then you are responsible for 2% of the taxes, insurance and maintenance of the entire center. Under the full service gross lease, the tenant does not pay for any of these expenses; instead, they are included in the rental rate.

■ **Tenant Improvements**

When you lease a space, you will usually have to make some improvements to it before you are ready to open for business. These include putting tiles on the floor, painting the walls, hanging lights. Make sure to look at the space and have your contractor do an estimate as to how much money it will cost to "build out" or prepare the space for your specific use.

Often times you can negotiate a tenant improvement allowance from the landlord. This is simply an allowance that the landlord gives you as money to be spent on improving the space. An example would be $10 per square foot to be provided by the landlord. Be sure to ask for some type of allowance as more times than not you can get something. Note that you will not always be able to get the tenant improvement allowance in cash. A common fallback is receive free rent at the beginning of the term as the allowance for the tenant improvements.

While some people prefer to skip the letter of intent and go directly to the lease, we recommend that you negotiate the basic deal points up front. By doing this you gain a general agreement on the deal points. Then both parties can focus on the legal details within the lease.

B. The Lease itself :

You should read and understand each provision in the lease before signing. If you are not comfortable with reading legal documents, we recommend that you hire an attorney to review the lease for you. Remember that an attorney can cost you a lot of money if they are not given specific instructions as to what you want them to do. We recommend that you hire an attorney and instruct them to simply review the lease and make recommendations only in those areas that are of particular concern. This will keep your legal advice bill to a manageable size.

Important Legal Clauses:

While there are many standard provisions in a lease there, are a few additional provisions with which we highly recommend you become familiar. These provisions preserve your location's strength and subsequently, your business's success. Here's a list of additional clauses:

Non-Competition Clause:

This clause is very important to your business. You have spent a significant amount of time looking for the right location and now it is time to protect your investment. The non-competition clause is intended to prevent the landlord from leasing space in the shopping center where your space is to a tenant that has the same type of business as yours. For example , in your case you are going to open another wild bird store. You would want your second landlord to agree in writing that he/she would not allow another bird store to open in the center. Industry examples show that when direct competitors are located in the same shopping center they tend to split or share the total business available. Without such a clause, the sales of your business may be cut in half.

No Substantial Changes to the Shopping Center:

This clause also protects your location. It serves to prevent the lessor from constructing a building in front of your space which would significantly affect your visibility and business success. The clause should restrict the landlord from deviating from shopping center plans (an addendum you should attach to the lease) without your permission. The result is that your visibility cannot be blocked, and access cannot be changed etc.

There are many industry examples in which a tenant is located in an in-line space and a pad is built in front of the space that blocks visibility from the street and ultimately results in a decrease in sales. There have also been examples where an access point that was very convenient, was closed or relocated. By negotiating a "no substantial changes" clause into your lease, you can protect yourself against such events

Anchor Goes Dark:

If you are part of a center that is anchored by a large grocery store or mass merchandiser, then one reason you made the decision to locate there was because of the drawing power of the anchor. But if the anchor for some reason closes or moves, the center immediately becomes less vibrant and as a result, your sales will probably drop substantially. A provision should be added to your lease that basically states that if there is an anchor tenant and that anchor tenant closes or moves, then you have the right to terminate your lease. While many landlords do not like this clause, it is important for you to pursue it.

Lease Recognition:

This clause says that if the shopping center has a mortgage then the lessor agrees to obtain from the mortgagee a letter evidencing the mortgagee's recognition of your lease. The letter should say that the mortgagee will recognize your lease during the primary term or any extensions of your lease. The reason this letter is important is that it protects your lease terms and rights in the event that a loan on the building is defaulted on.

The above provisions are important in preserving the location you have selected.

Going into great detail over legal provisions is outside the scope of this book. As a result we strongly recommend that you spend ample time learning more about basic contract law and the provisions that make up a lease and or purchase agreement. Discuss all matters concerning your location and your lease with your business advisor, accountant and/or attorney before making any business decision.

Demographic Resources:

Wild Bird Feeding Industry
P. O. Box 502
West End , NC 27376
888-839-1237
Tshays@wbfi.org
www.wbfi.org

Department of the Interior
National Survey of Hunting, Fishing and Wildlife Watching
Fish and Wildlife Service
Washington DC

Demographic Reports:
Area reports are usually provided by the rental agent for any property you are considering to lease.

Appendix B

Trade Area Form

Trade Area #: _____ Description _____

Location _____

Ref Intersection: _____

Generators:
(include the names of the major tenants, the size and the vibrancy level)

1. _____

2. _____

3. _____

4. _____

Traffic:
(Include the traffic counts on the major streets, the patterns, the speed limit and the character)

_____

_____

_____

Road Configuration:
(Focus on the primary street and discuss medians, center turn lanes, number of lanes etc.)

_____

_____

Seasonability:
(Note any changes in the population as they relate to the seasons)

_____

_____

Day Parts
(Note the days of the week and the times of day when the Trade Area appears to be most vibrant.

_____

_____

Appendix C
Check List

☐ Decide on a territory to research

☐ Obtain maps

☐ Study those maps

☐ Visit the Chamber of Commerce and Department of Transportation

☐ Visit & draw Trade Area maps
- Include
  - ☐ Generators (Type and Name)
  - ☐ Competition
  - ☐ National Players
  - ☐ Major cross streets

☐ Complete the Trade Area form

☐ Prioritize the Trade Areas

☐ Look for sites within the top ranking Trade Areas.

☐ Order demographics for potential sites

☐ Pick a site.

☐ Create a letter of intent.

☐ Negotiate the terms of the deal

☐ Close the deal.

☐ Obtain a copy of " Layout and Design manual from NAIWBS."

☐ Layout and Design your store

☐ Open for business

 **Marketing Brief**

The Series:

1. Gearing up for Greater Sales

150 pages of help during times when things need a boost.
Available from Amazon.com

2. Fall and Winter Wild Bird Feed Sale

Based on 41 years of experience in holding wild bird feed sales
Available from Amazon.com

3. Newspaper Advertising Workbook

Don't start advertising until after you read this manual.
Available from Amazon.com

4. Location, Location, Location

How the big boys do it.
Available from Amazon.com

5. The Wilkerson Formula

How to make $9,000 on a weekend Sidewalk Sale
Pending Publication near the end of April 2016